Hero Dog Stories

16 Amazing Tales of

Love and Courage

Jennifer Ogden

Table of Contents

Introduction

As a dog owner, I know what an important part of the family a dog becomes. When I was young I would play cards with my dog when no one else would play with me. Of course he didn't do anything but sitting there staring at me like I was stupid, but he never offered to move. Through the years I have owned several different dogs of all different types of breeds. Each dog had a different personality, but always won a special place in my heart.

There has always been one thing that has remained the same through my many years of owning dogs, a day is a very loyal friend. He is there when no one else is. He will make you smile with the goofy things he does and he may even make you a little mad from time to time but no matter what he is there. There is no way you could stay mad at your little pooch for too long even when he strung toilet paper all over the house while you were out because he was boarded. Next time that happens just consider it a sign of his love and affection.

My Bassett Hound Barney is as simple as they come. He isn't the smartest of dogs, but he sure makes me smile. He sits around most days with those sad eyes, but the moment you talk to him he lights up. He perks up and runs to me like he hasn't seen me in a week. Poor Barney, he loves to have his belly rubbed but just can't quite figure out how to roll over. So he will lay the front half of his body down while the back half remains in the air. It is the funniest thing. I have to help him roll on over.

Now Cupcake my little Chihuahua mix is somewhat of a brat. She doesn't like Barney to have any of her attention. She can be rotten, but she is truly a very sweet dog. Although, when she has had enough of your affection she will get up and go to her bed. I really enjoy snuggling with her when she lets me. I love both of my dogs dearly and that is why I decided to write this book. All of these stories are true examples of how loving and loyal a dog can be.

Please note that due to copyright issues I was unable to get pictures of the actual dogs mentioned in each story, but I have done my best to provide pictures of the hero dog's breed so you can see what the hero dog looks like.

Wishing you and your dog friends the very best,

Jennifer

<u>Honey</u>

Michael Bosch was a 63-year-old real estate man. He really wanted a cocker spaniel puppy, and had been waiting on one for more than a year. Finally, the wait was over. The Marin Humane Society had received Honey because her owner could no longer afford to care for her. Michael was thrilled!

Michael's wife was traveling a lot with her job, and he recently had heart surgery. So he adopted Honey to keep him active and be a trusted companion.The cocker spaniel puppy was in the back of her cage at the shelter when Michael saw her for the first time. She was shaking with fear. Michael asked one of the workers if he could hold her. As soon as he held her in his arms, she stopped shaking.

She was only five months old, and longed to be held and loved.

Michael took Honey outside, set her on the ground and threw a ball for her. She came racing back and landed in Michael's lap. That was all it took for Michael. He filled out the paperwork, and took his new cocker spaniel puppy home. Honey was Michael's shadow for the first day, but he didn't mind! It was instant love between Michael and Honey.

On November 2, 2005 Honey walked along with Michael and got into his SUV. He had only had Honey for 2 weeks, but the two of them were already best friends. He allowed his perky cocker spaniel puppy to go with him to run some errands. He hopped in the car, and Honey joined him without hesitation.

She sat proudly in the passenger seat awaiting their voyage. Michael lives in the remote hills of San Rafael, California. This area is thick with huge redwood trees. His driveway is located on top of a hill, and there is barely enough room for one car to fit through. At the end there is a very steep drop off.

He backed up slowly and was looking for oncoming traffic. Suddenly a flash of light impaired his vision. He used his hand to shelter his eyes from the sunlight. That's when he felt the left rear end of the SUV drop off. He knew immediately that his car had encountered the steep edge. The SUV began to tumble. He had forgotten to put on his safety belt, which resulted in him being tossed about the SUV as it plummeted to the ground. He could hear branches snapping. Without notice there was a large crunching noise.

An enormous branch came through the roof of his SUV. The branch struck his legs and chest, and impelled his dashboard. He and Honey were in an upside down position in the SUV. He knew instantly that the branch had him pinned in. He felt the pain within his chest.

Michael tried to free himself from the branch, but it was no use. He could tell that there was something wrong with his legs. He was able to retrieve his cell phone, and frantically dialed 911. It was no use, as his cell phone did not have a signal. Michael and his trusted cocker spaniel puppy were now stuck at the bottom of a ravine, with no signal on his cell phone to call for help!

His closest neighbor was a quarter-mile uphill, and there was no reason she would go looking for

Michael. The SUV had fallen 40 feet down into a very secluded ravine.

Michael's only hope was sending his trusted companion for help. He helped Honey escape from a window in the SUV. She quickly ran up the hill, and sat in a location where the neighbors would see her when they came home that evening. Robin Allen spotted the dog, and got out to investigate. Honey directed Robin to the scene of the wreck.

After waiting in pain for 8 hours Michael was finally extracted by firefighters from the vehicle. They had to use the Jaws of Life to strip away the car metal to reach him. Michael's pulse was beginning to weaken from hanging upside down for so long. He was flown to Santa Rosa Memorial Hospital. They treated him for 5 broken bones, severe leg injuries and he was later transferred to Kaiser Permanente Medical Center. His legs had been severely crushed between the steering wheel, and the large branch that impaled his SUV's dashboard.

While he was in the hospital some of Michael's coworkers brought Honey to visit him. Honey was overjoyed to see Michael. She gave him a warm greeting, and covered him with doggy kisses. Seeing Honey made Michael feel better. She had only been in his life for 2 weeks, but she already meant so much to him. If she had not gone for help, Michael's injuries could have been fatal! Luckily, Honey realized that they were in danger, and did not hesitate to retrieve some help. Honey saved Michael's life, but Michael also saved Honey's by adopting her. You could say the two of them were destined to be together!

<u>Lilly</u>

Lilly is an 8 year old Pit Bull Terrier. She lives in Shirley, Massachusetts with her owner, Christine, who believes Lilly is a true hero. On May 4, 2012 Christine and her trusty Pit Bull Terrier were enjoying their daily walk when Christine suddenly fell to the ground.

The situation turned from bad to worse, as Christine fell upon a train track, blacked out and a train was speeding towards her! Lilly heard the approaching train, and began trying to remove Christine from the tracks. Lilly tugged and pulled, desperately trying to get Christine out of the train's path.

"The engineer, the only witness, told police he saw the Pit Bull Terrier frantically pulling at a woman as he drew closer. He did everything he could to stop the train before reaching them.

Suddenly there was a loud thump as the train came to a screeching halt. The engineer was sick with the thought that he may have just hit both Lilly and Christine. Frightened and upset, the engineer leapt out of the train to see what remained of the heroic dog and his owner. Lilly had just managed to pull Christine away before the train reached her!

Christine suffered no injuries but Lilly was not so fortunate. Her right front leg was completely stripped of all the skin and muscle, and she suffered a fractured hip bone.

The heroic Pit Bull Terrier was taken to the Angell Animal Medical center in Boston, where the doctors made the decision to amputate her leg. They replaced the hip bone with steel plates to give her more support. After several months of physical therapy, doctors predicted that Lilly would be able to walk again.

Lilly made a full recovery and is at home where she belongs watching over Christine. Christian feels fortunate that her trusted companion was with her that day. Her Pit Bull Terrier will forever be a hero for being brave enough to risk her own life. This is a true example of how loyal a dog can be.

The Legendary Balto

A Siberian Husky named Balto was born in 1919. He was a natural sled dog from a young age, and later become known as a hero worldwide. In 1925, there was a large outbreak of a diphtheria epidemic in Nome, Alaska. This deadly disease was killing people quickly. The only hope that the people of Nome had, was a life-saving antidote located in Anchorage, which was over 1,000 miles away. The town was in danger of being wiped out if they did not receive the antidote soon.

Alaska's extremely cold weather had caused the engine of the only aircraft that could quickly deliver the vaccine, to freeze. The people of Nome considered alternative ways of getting the serum, but with the extremely frigid weather they didn't have many choices. Once the serum left Anchorage by train and arrived in Nenana, it would have to be carried the rest of the way by several different teams of dog sleds. The team of dogs had to face a snow storm with temperatures as low as -23°F, along with difficult winds.

Balto led a team of dogs that were driven by Gunnar Kaasen. The determined Siberian Husky and his team would drive the serum part of the way to Nome. Their journey began on February 2, 1925. The lead dog has the most strenuous job on the team, as he is in charge of steering them away from danger. Balto, being the robust Siberian Husky that he was, navigated his way through a whiteout environment that made it impossible to see even a few feet away.

Balto and his team ran their leg of the journey in the dark. They were supposed to hand the serum to another team, but when they arrived at the drop spot the other team was sleeping. Kaasen then made the choice to carry the serum the rest of the way into Nome.

Balto and the rest of the team covered almost 700 miles in extremely treacherous weather. They did this in just under 5 days, which was truly amazing since it took most teams about 25 days to cover that same distance!

When they arrived in Nome, the people wanted to praise Kaasen as a hero, but he told them Balto deserved the credit. Without Balto the trip would not have been made. He was able to navigate through weather conditions that no other man or dog could have!

Some of the other dog team members were upset with the attention that Balto received from everyone, especially President Calvin Coolidge. People all over the nation loved the story of the brave Siberian Huskey who saved Nome, and he was considered the hero of the serum run. Balto and Kassen received worldwide fame. In New York City's Central Park there is a statue to honor Balto. He was present during the presentation of his statue in New York.

On the monument it reads:

"Dedicated to the indomitable spirit of the sled dogs that relayed antitoxin six hundred miles over rough ice, across treacherous waters, through Arctic

blizzards from Nenana to the relief of stricken Nome in the winter of 1925."

Endurance · Fidelity · Intelligence

Balto died in 1933 but his remains were preserved by a taxidermist and are on display at the Cleveland Museum of Natural History. In 1955, they made an animated movie about him and his famous journey. Balto team saved a whole town from an outbreak of disease. He became a national hero for pushing through conditions that even a man couldn't make it through!

<u>Buddy</u>

It's said that a dog is a "Man's best friend." Many people would agree by saying a dog is not just a dog he is a family member. A dog can be trained to do many different things. Some can roll over, sit pretty, act dead, or dance in a circle. Dogs can even be trained to save lives. This is just one story about the amazing things a dog can do!

Joe Stalnaker lives in the busy city of Scottsdale, Arizona. Being independent was difficult for Joe. Several years ago, he was injured during a military training accident. He suffered a head injury that has caused him to experience frequent seizures. His seizures come without warning and require medical attention. Joe became worried that one day

33

he would suffer a seizure that would result in severe injuries. The type of seizures that Joe experiences needs to be addressed by medical professionals. If he doesn't get the medical attention he needs it could cost him his life.

Joe managed to live on his own for a while, but he started experiencing more and more seizure activity. It was important for Joe to seek medical attention quickly when he had these seizures because they could claim his life. So he decided it was time to be proactive about seeking a way to live on his own, and get the medical help he needs when a seizure occurs. Joe found a place in Michigan called Paws with a Cause. They train dogs to help people with disabilities like Joe's, to live independent lives.

They agreed to train a dog to call 911 when Joe began to have a seizure. Their process was not easy. He had to fill out lots of paperwork and it took months to find a suitable dog for Joe. Joe would have to also commit to working with his service dog regularly to keep up his special skills. Joe was determined to live by himself. He was willing to do whatever it took!

Joe traveled from Arizona to Michigan to pick up an 8 week old German Shepard he named Buddy. Joe and Buddy became instant friends. Joe found it easy to work with Buddy on his training for dialing 911. He was a very clever German Shepard. Joe knew that a seizure could happen at any time and wanted to make sure Buddy was ready. Buddy was instructed to push programmed buttons with his teeth until a 911 operator came on the line.

Joe and Buddy were inseparable. Everywhere Joe went Buddy would be right by his side in case Joe had a seizure. They practiced often, but Joe had hoped all of their practicing would help Buddy make that 911 call when he was experiencing an actual seizure. Everyone always says, "Practice makes perfect!" Only time would tell if that was true for Buddy!

On September 10, 2008, Joe had a seizure and fell on the floor, unconscious. He was suffering a major seizure that required immediate medical attention. Although, Buddy had never had to put his training into use before, Buddy did not hesitate. The German Shepard raced quickly and retrieved the phone to dial 911 just like he was taught.

"Hello, this is 911. Hello… Can you hear me? Is there somebody there you can give the phone to," asked the dispatcher, Chris Trott. Obviously, Buddy couldn't talk in human words, but he made the urgency of the situation clear. Buddy whined and howled in response to the questions the dispatcher asked.

Responders arrived at Joe's house within 3 minutes. When officers arrived, Chris was still on the phone with the German Shepard. He was able to hear Buddy in the background barking loudly. Officers found Joe blacked out on the floor suffering from a seizure. He was taken to the hospital immediately where he spent two days making a full recovery from his seizure.

Both the responders and dispatchers were in disbelief that Buddy, the German Shepard, had saved his owner's life by making that vital call to 911. None of them had ever witnessed this before. Buddy was known as a hero, not only to Joe, but also to people around the nation. His remarkable training paid off and saved Joe's life.

Joe's address is now flagged in the Scottsdale 911 system so that responders will know that there is a trained service dog that is able to make 911 calls. Buddy is more than just a dog to Joe.

Joe said, *"He looks after me from the time I get up until the time I go to bed. If he thinks I have been in bed too long he will nibble on my fingers to wake me up. He is simply amazing. He has given me back my independence. He's my world. He's my best friend, no question. He's always there, and I just hope I can be as good to him as he's been to me."*

Buddy is certainly the type of dog anyone would want to have around when an emergency occurs. Buddy has made over 6 different calls to 911 for Joe while he was having a seizure.

Joe and Buddy continue to live in the busy town of Scottsdale, Arizona. They take daily walks, play fetch, and live a normal everyday life. But Joe knows that when an emergency occurs he has Buddy there to take care of him. They have a friendship that goes beyond "Man's best friend.

Without Buddy, Joe would not be able to live an independent life. Buddy gives him the freedom that Joe has so desperately wanted after his accident. He is grateful to Paws for claws and the training they did with Buddy.

<u>Maya</u>

Pit Bulls are usually not thought of as heroes. Most people are scared of them because of the bad reputation they have received over the years. This story may make you reconsider making a pre-determined judgment about the Pit Bull breed.

Angela made the decision to get a dog for her family. She visited the Humane Society in Silicon Valley, and looked at many dogs. However, it was a 3 month old Pit Bull mix that won her heart. Angela decided to name the newest addition to her family, Maya.

Angela and her son adored Maya. In the years that followed, Maya never showed any aggression towards them or those who visited their home. Life was good with Maya, as she proved to be the dog that Angela had fallen in love with.

On Father's Day 2007, Angela was returning to her home when she was unexpectedly greeted by an unwanted intruder. She was being robbed, and was completely overwhelmed with what was happening. The robber shoved Angela in the door. He then proceeded to strangle her to prevent any screaming.

Angela managed to make two successful cries during her attack. Thankfully, this alerted Maya. She immediately understood Angela's cries for help. The brave Pit Bull came to her owners aid by growling. When the intruder ignored her growling tactics, Maya wasted no more time. She sunk her razor sharp teeth into the unlucky intruder. While struggling to fight off the dog, the man lost his hold on Angela and she was able to escape her attacker's assault. She scrambled to her feet, and began helping Maya attack the intruder.

Shortly after Maya's attack began, the intruder realized he had chosen the wrong house to break into. He had also misjudged Maya and Angela's ability to defend themselves. The defeated intruder made a quick decision to make his exit.

Angela ran after the intruder, and was able to view his license plate number. She repeated it several times in her head as she made a frantic call to 911. Maya, the heroic Pit Bull, had blood on her face from the robber, which allowed police the opportunity to take a DNA swab. It was difficult for the police to obtain the DNA sample because Maya was still very upset about the attack. She did not want to let the police near her.

The detectives were able to get a DNA match from the blood that was collected. It came back as Anthony Easley, 37, who had been convicted of similar crimes before. The police asked Angela to come down to the station to help identify the intruder.

They place several men in a lineup, and sure enough Angela pick Anthony out as her assailant. This gave them enough evidence to put Anthony behind bars for a long time.

Maya was not only a local hero, she was also named the 2008 National Dog Day Hero by the Animal Miracle Foundation.

River

In Ipswich, Australia, lives a family who hails their dog River a true hero. River is an 18 month old mixed Red Cattle dog who has a sense of urgency when it comes to harm around the farm. Cattle dogs are bred to watch over a herd. The red cattle dog originated from Australia. These dogs are bred to drive cattle over long distances and rough terrains.

Kaylee, who was 2, and Michelle, who was 7, were heading outside to play on their swing set. While in route to their play set they spotted a snake, and proceeded to let out a scream. Their trusty dog River came between the rearing eastern brown snake and the children. The eastern brown snake is highly venomous. River saved the lives of Kaylee and Michelle and jeopardized her own.

River was successful in killing the snake, but not before the snake sunk his fangs into the brave red cattle dog. River was taken to the vet in Booval where they found a snake bite on his back leg. He then underwent anti-venom. His total treatment cost over $2000.

Kaylee and Michelle witness the attack and have been deeply traumatized by this event. Both of them asked questions about what had happened to their loving dog River. The girl's mother, Catherine Lynch said, "This is an important reminder to parents that we should check the yard for snakes before allowing children to go out and play! It's a lesson for all us, of what can happen, and how easily it can happen."

Catherine was in the front yard gardening while the girl's decided to play on the swing set. The snake measured 70 cm long. They took the dead snake with them to the vet so that it could be correctly identified and River could receive the best treatment. This event could have ended a lot worse. The family is very thankful River reached the snake first.

Matt Harley, who is a snake handler said, "that the brown snake can reach up to 1.5m long. They are tan to almost black and are very quick to strike compared to other snakes. The snake that River killed was relatively young, but even this snake could cause fatalities. If you encounter a snake it is best to back up very slowly. If you happen to be standing over it, be very still and move away as slow as possible. It is the movement that gets the snake's attention and causes them to strike. If you are bitten by a snake make sure you get first aid immediately. "

Ms. Lynch the veterinarian who cared for River said that she responded well to anti-venom treatment, and returned home to the Lynch family after she made a full recovery. River will forever be a hero to the Lynch family. She saved the lives of their daughters and risked her own.

<u>Rocky</u>

When you hear the name Rocky, what do you think of? You may think of the famous Rocky Balboa who was a boxer. The people in Edmonton, Alberta have a very different picture of Rocky. Rocky to them is a four-legged hero who saved the lives of two girls.

It was an icy Easter Sunday morning when Adam Shaw was out taking a walk with his wife, kids, and their dog Rocky. They were walking along the North Saskatchewan River. Rocky is an 8-year-old Labrador Retriever-Husky mix who enjoys walking and playing with his family. Even at 8 years old, which is almost old age for a dog, Rocky remains very active.

Adam was walking on a bridge over the river when he heard screams. He looked down at the icy river below, and spotted one girl in the freezing water. The girl's sister was trying her best to rescue her out of the life threatening water. Adam told his wife to call 911, while he and Rocky raced down the embankment to where the girls were. By the time they reached them, both girls were in the water.

Adam and his trusty Labrador Retriever mix had to work quickly, as the girls were in danger of losing their lives. Adam was able to retrieve one of the girls, who was named Krymzen, from the icy water. However, her sister , Samara, was being carried downstream. Samara was now 4 to 5 feet from the edge of the ice, her head was bobbing in and out of the water, and Adam felt the sense of urgency. The situation was getting worse by the minute.

Adam asked Samara if she could swim, but she replied, "I can't move my arms or legs." He tried to throw Rocky's leash to her, but it wasn't long enough. The closer he and Rocky got to Samara, the more the ice began to give away. A moment later, the ice broke. Adam and Rocky fell into the water.

Adam started to get really scared, because he now realized how cold the water really was. Adam's adrenaline was pumping, and he had to save Samara. As she drifted further downstream, Adam tried frantically to get out of the water so he could race to her. Both he and Rocky tried pulling them back to shore, but the ice was so thin it kept breaking away.

Finally, Rocky was able to get his front paws on a block of ice, and Adam pushed his back legs up. The Labrador Retriever was now standing on the ice.

Adam used the leash, and Rocky to pull himself out of the icy river. Samara was now 50 to 60 yards farther down the river. Adam realized that he was going to need a better plan, otherwise he and Rocky would become victims as well. Samara was still struggling to stay afloat in the frigid water. Adam and Rocky ran as close as they could to Samara, but she was still out of reach.

Adam placed the leash around Rocky, and urged him to get into the water. He instructed Samara to try to get a hold of the Labrador Retrievers leash. He gave Samara hope by telling her if she was able to grab Rocky's leash, they could pull her up to the block of ice. Rocky did as instructed, and swam to the girl. Samara was then able to grab the leash with both hands.

Adam called for Rocky to swim back. Rocky towed Samara back to safety through the crumbling ice. Adam was able to grab Samara's arm. He dragged both the girl and his brave Labrador Retriever away from the water's edge. He didn't want anyone slipping back into the water. Adam tried to carry Samara up the embankment, but it was too steep. The three of them, worn to exhaustion, sat down at the edge of the river to rest.

Unexpectedly, Adam's cell phone began to ring. He couldn't believe his phone still worked after being introduced to the frigid water. It was the emergency rescue team telling him to stay put, that they would be there within minutes. A rescue crew arrived shortly after, and took the sisters to the hospital. After being thoroughly examined, both girls were medically cleared, and sent home to recover from their traumatic event.

The two girls, -- Krymzen, 10, and Samara, 9— were out sledding that afternoon in the park. The sled slid down off the snow bank, and skidded onto the frozen river. The girls went together to retrieve it. The ice gave away, and that's when Samara slipped in. While Krymzen tried relentlessly to save her sister, a piece of ice beneath her gave away.

Rocky had always been an "adventurous" dog, who liked to go in and out of the water. He had always surprised his owners with the way he could jump off high surfaces in the water and swim back with no problem. Adam had no worries about Rocky when the dog entered the river. Adam knew that his Labrador Retriever had the ability to swim back to him through the icy water without difficulty. His concern was that Samara could not use her arms to grab onto Rocky's leash.

Adam was quoted as saying, "I think he knew something out of the ordinary was going on. After it all happened, we were sitting on the shore and he's a pretty active dog, he's usually running around and stuff, but he came and sat down beside me and the girls and didn't move."

The mother of the girls, Miranda Wagner, was so thankful to Adam and Rocky for heroically saving her two daughters. "I just want to give him a big hug and tell him he's my hero. If he wasn't there I wouldn't have my girls," Wagner said. "Doctors said two more minutes and Samara would have been gone."

The people of Edmonton deemed Rocky and Adam heroes for saving the two girls from the icy river. They could have also easily become victims of the ice if they had not been able to scramble out of the freezing water. The firemen honored Adam with a fireman's hat, and Rocky received a giant rawhide bone. The heroic Labrador Retriever was so excited, that he grabbed the bone from the Fire Chief's hand before the plastic wrapper could be removed.

Rocky and Adam will forever be heroes to Samara, Krymzen, and their mom Miranda. Each of them played an important role in ensuring the girls were recovered from the water safely. This story could have had a very tragic ending, but Rocky was not frightened of the icy water. They worked together to ensure there was a happy ending.

Saving Grace

Fostering a dog can be very rewarding. Alice Zeitz from Newfane, New York is dedicated to fostering dogs who need permanent homes.. She has fostered more than 100 dogs through the Akron Canine Rescued Angels program. Fostering a dog is where you agree to keep the canine until a suitable owner comes along. This gives the dog one-on-one care that they need. Plus, the dog doesn't have to stay in a cage all day at an animal shelter. On this particular occasion, Alice had chosen a black mixed breed dog to foster named Grace.

When Alice agreed to foster the dog she didn't realize how very special Grace would become to her! When the rescue center found her, Grace was tied to a stop sign with a litter of puppies. Luckily, the rescue center brought her to their facility. Alice wanted to be a hero to Grace by finding her a good home. Little did she know that this dog would end up saving her!

It was only days until Christmas, and Alice's house was buzzing with activity. She had started laundry in the basement of her home, and returned to the upstairs to be with her children and fiance. Her kids were anticipating the holidays as most children do! Alice and her family had become quite fond of Grace. She was fitting in perfectly, but Alice knew that was the hardest part of fostering a dog. You can't keep all of them! She realized that Grace would have to find a suitable home soon. Still, there was something so special about Grace that Alice was drawn to.

Alice had only been upstairs for a short period of time before Grace started pacing back and forth. Alice could tell that she was very disturbed by something in the basement. Finally, Grace began to bark. That is when Alice knew something had to be wrong. Grace wasn't the type of dog who barked for no reason. So she followed Grace to the basement, and found the washer surrounded by smoke. The washer had caught on fire, and Grace had detected the smoke. Dogs have a very keen sense of smell, and this heroic canine beat the smoke detector! It had not gone off yet, but Grace had known there was a fire!

Because of Grace's great sense of smell, there was no severe damage to the home or family. This made Alice realize how special Grace truly was. Alice

67

adopted Grace because of her bravery that saved her family and home.

Alice had felt a special connection with Grace before this event had occurred, but this made that connection even stronger. Alice continues to foster rescued dogs. Grace herself could be considered a hero to our four-legged friends in need. She has found hundreds of homes for abandoned animals. Alice said, "A lot of people have this image that shelter dogs or dogs in rescue are all bad, that they're in the rescue because they did something wrong, and that is totally not the case. It's the same with Rottweilers and pit bulls. A lot of people have the image that they are nasty dogs. We have a saying, 'Judge the deed, not the breed,' because it's all in how they are raised."

<u>Napoleon</u>

Dogs are talented in different ways! This story is unique in a way because the most unlikely breed of dog, took a heroic swim to save the life of an even more unlikely friend! When you talk about a dog that is a good swimmer you may think of a Golden Retriever, not an English Bulldog!

Bulldogs are not good swimmers because of the size of their head, chest and small backend. This is a combination that usually causes swimming to be a real challenge for them. Swimming is such a problem for English Bulldogs that owners are made aware of the problem when they purchase or adopt them.

Napoleon and his owner were out taking their morning stroll. Typically, Napoleon was a very well-behaved and obedient English bulldog, but something caught Napoleon's attention that morning. He sped across the road and jumped in the lake. This was very out of character for him and his owner, Alexandra Breuer, was shocked. Actually, Breuer was pretty mad at Napoleon for being so disobedient.

Before Breuer could scold Napoleon too much, he was dragging a burlap sack out of the water. At first, Breuer thought it was a bag of garbage, but then she heard meowing coming from the bag. There were six kittens all together, but two had already died. Amazingly Napoleon heard the kittens struggling and raced to their aid.

Alexandra and Napoleon cared for the kittens until they were old enough to be adopted. When they were ready, Alexandra took them to a local pet adoption center where they could be placed in homes. When Napoleon, the English Bulldog, arrived at the adoption center with his rescue kittens, everyone took time to give him the heroic treatment that he deserved.

Napoleon was especially brave to rescue the kitten from the water because he could have easily drowned. This story proves that we should never underestimate a dog's ability! No matter their shape or size.

<u>Moti</u>

A five year old German shepherd name Moti, came to his owner's rescue during gunfire. Some dogs would shy away from gunshots, but Moti didn't cower down. He sprung into action to save the lives of his family.

It was late one Friday night in the town of Florence, Pennsylvania. Harshad and Mital Patel owned a small shop in town. The Patels, their two daughters, and their German Sheppard were at the shop that evening. It was like any other evening. Many costumers had visited that day. The darkness filled the street outside, and that is when a masked gunman made his appearance in the Patels shop.

The Patels were stunned, and feared for the safety of their daughters. Mital knew instantly what was happening. She pushed the panic button to alert local police. The masked robber held a gun to Mital. He demanded she open the cash register and give him all the money. Harshad was about ready to give Moti a command to attack. However, before Harshap could call out the command the brave German Shepherd leapt into action.

All 114 pounds of Moti lunged over the counter, and started barking at the masked gunman. The robber was stunned by the appearance of the dog. Moti had not been in the gunman's sight when he approached the counter. The German Sheppard did not like the tone of the robber's voice, or the fear that his owners were expressing. Moti made a quick appearance because of this. The gunman realized

Moti had met business, so he took the cowardly way out. He pointed the gun at Moti and shot, while fleeing the store.

The Patels realized that their German Sheppard had been shot, and they rushed him to the veterinarian. The vet took an x-ray, which showed that the bullet had gone through Moti's neck. It missed his throat, but landed on his shoulder. Moti was rushed into emergency surgery to try to recover the bullet, but the vet was unable to retrieve it. The bullet still remains lodged in Moti's shoulder.

If Moti had not been so quick to scare the robber off, this could have been a very different story. The Patels realized what an amazing and heroic dog Moti was. The masked gunman is still at large, but

Moti has received special treatment from his family for his heroic deeds.

"Good meal, good steak. He gets everything good now. More than he needs!" said Harshad. Moti goes to the shop with the Patels daily, and takes his job very seriously. If he feels like there is something out-of-place he springs to his feet.

Tank and Muck, The Doggy Duo

Living next door to a friend is always fun and exciting. Dogs feel this way as well. A Rottweiler named Tank was best friends with his next door cross breed pal Muck. Muck and Tank were always spotted hanging out together. Not only did they enjoy playing, they also got in trouble from time to time.

It was a quiet December afternoon in Mackay, Australia. Like usual, Tank and Muck were outside playing. However, 2-year-old Max Hillier joined the doggy duo that day. Before long the trio set off on a journey. Tank had a habit of following Max, as the devoted Rottweiler was very protective of him. While Muck was used to following Tank everywhere, so he tagged along as well.

83

Georgie Hillier, Max's mother, thought that Max was out back playing with Tank in the yard. Little did she know that Max had actually wandered off with their Rottweiler, and the neighbor's dog. Georgie had not heard a peep out of Max, and began to worry. She went to the back yard to check on him, but could not find Max or their dog Tank.

Georgie, like any mother, felt a strong sense of urgency to find her son. She searched everywhere inside and out, but Max was nowhere to be found. She began searching for Max by car, as she was certain that he had wandered off. Suddenly, she discovered Tank. He was running around the dam anxiously. The Rottweiler was wet, and covered in moss from the dam. Panic began to set in, as Georgie knew Tank was anxious for a reason. He was all wet, and this made her think he had gone into the dam to rescue Max. However, Max was nowhere in sight.

At this point Georgie knew she had to get someone else involved. If he was in the dam she needed to get help quickly. She frantically drove back to her house and phoned 911.

Meanwhile, a neighbor reported that she heard barking coming from the dam beside her house. When she went to investigate the barking dogs, she found Tank hovering over Max, while Muck was protecting the space between Max and the dam. Muck was attempting to keep Max from reentering the murky water.

Georgie was desperate to have her son back. She raced around the dam calling out Max's name. The neighbor had found the two dogs and Max, muddy but alive. When the neighbor heard Georgie yelling for them, she returned Max to his mother.

Emergency workers arrived at the dam. They examined the spot where Max was found. There were very noticeable drag marks, and officers say it was clear that Max was pulled from the water by one of the heroic dogs. It became obvious that Tank had pulled Max from the water, and Muck distracted him from reentering.

Max could have drowned, if not for this heroic doggy duo. The Hilliers feel very blessed to have Max back with them alive and well. They also didn't realize what an exceptional dog they have. Tank and his pal Muck have received some very special treatment for their heroic actions.

Tank and his best friend Muck were awarded the Purple Cross Award from the RSPCA in November 2007. Michael Beattie a representative from the RSPCA said, "A dog's protective nature and sixth sense should never be underestimated. Obviously, in this particular case, the dog realized that something was going wrong. And that young Max was obviously in distress and each dog decided to do what he had to do. The award is given out to an animal that has, in a way, gone above and beyond the call of duty and basically risked their lives to save a human."

Each dog received a medallion, certificate, and a huge bone to snack on! Tank and Muck continue to enjoy all the attention that they have earned. Tank was rescued from the pound by the Hilliers. Now they consider him a hero for saving their son, but had the Hilliers not adopted Tank as a puppy, he wouldn't have a home. Thanks to them Tank got a chance to show that he is a valuable canine to have around.

Things have quieted down for Muck and Tank, but this duo continues to be the best of friends. Perhaps they are waiting for the next big adventure to come along. Either way, these two pals have earned their keep!

<u>Kabang</u>

Ruby Bunggal could be considered a hero herself, as she took in a stray puppy off the streets of Zambanga in the Philippines. She named her new companion Kabang, but little did she know that her four legged friend would become an international hero. Kabang is a shepherd and Aspin mix.

Ruby's daughter, Dina, was only nine years old. She was watching over her cousin Princess Diansing, who was only three at the time. It was a busy day in December 2011 when Dina and Princess attempted to cross a very busy street. Kabang was accompanying the duo that day. Dina misjudged a break in traffic, and stepped into the path of an oncoming motorcycle. However, Kabang did not hesitate, as she knew the girls were in danger. Kabang leaped in front of the motorcycle, and caused it to come to a screeching halt before hitting the girls.

Bystanders saw the crash, and all agreed that the girls would have been critically injured had Kabang not took quick action, and stepped in front of the motorcycle. The driver of the motorcycle and both girls only suffered from minor injuries. However, Kabang was trapped in the front end of the motorcycle, and was severely injured. Rescuers were able to get her loose from the wheel of the motorcycle, but Kabang quickly escaped the team of rescuers once she was freed. The brave canine was frightened from the traumatic event that just took place. Ruby knew that Kabang's wounds were fatal, and desperately hoped the dog would reappear. She wanted to get her heroic canine the medical attention that she so desperately needed.

Finally, two weeks after the accident had taken place, Kabang reappeared at the Bunggal home. It was simply amazing that Kabang had lived that long without medical attention. Ruby reportedly said, "The bones holding her upper snout were crushed, and we could not do anything to save it". Even though, Kabang's jaw could not be saved, Ruby refused to have the dog put down. Kabang had saved her daughter and cousin, and she was willing to do anything to give the heroic canine the best life possible.

Kabang's injuries to her upper jaw made it hard for her to eat. Other than that Kabang managed to live a normal life, and even had a litter of puppies.

However, a serious infection began in the area where Kabang's snout was torn from her face. The local vet gave the canine antibiotics, but she would need extensive facial surgery to survive. The open area was so large, and there was no way antibiotics alone could take care of it. Surgery would cost thousands of dollars, and the Bunggal family did not have that kind of money to spend. Ruby was heartbroken, and refused to put Kabang down.

In February 2012, a nurse from New York named Karen Kenngott, saw Kabang's story on the internet. She was drawn to Kabang's story, and wanted to help this heroic canine get the help she so desperately needed. Karen started an organization called "Care for Kabang," and also recruited the help of the Animal Welfare Coalition. With the two organizations on board, they were able to meet their fundraising goal within four weeks.

Kabang became an international hero during the organization's campaign to raise money to save her life. People were touched by the heroic canine, and were more than willing to help. This brought a lot of opportunities, as even more money was raised.

People traveled from all over the world just to have their picture taken with Kabang. In October 2012, Kabang underwent a specialized surgery in the United States at the William R. Pritchard Veterinary Medical Teaching Hospital. Upon her arrival to the facility, she was thoroughly evaluated.

During her evaluation, the doctors found that Kabang also had heartworms and a transmissible venereal tumor, which is a type of cancer. A week after she arrived at the clinic, Kabang started chemotherapy, and her surgery was postponed until March 2013.

Finally, two years after the wreck had occurred, Kabang underwent surgery, and it was a huge success! All of Kabang's surgery and treatment were paid for by donations from 47 different countries. Her total treatment came to $27,000. On June 8, 2013 Kabang returned to her family in the Philippines. She was given a big hero's welcome in her home town of Zamboanga. Today, Kabang lives a completely normal life. She does not need any medications.

Kabang won the hearts of people all over the world because of her heroic actions. Although, Her injuries were severe, she was able to make a full recovery. Karen's organization, along with the Animal

Welfare Coalition, ensured Kabang received the care that she needed. Kabang saved two lives, and the world came to gather to save her.

<u>Henry</u>

There is something magical about being in the great outdoors. Nature has so much to offer, and it is splendid when you get to spend the day outside. Many people choose to utilize natural resources in their daily lives. It's amazing to live off the land, and enjoy the beauty that surrounds us. This is the case for Frank Walker and his trusty chocolate Labrador retriever Henry.

Frank owns and lives on a 20 acre lot in Sango, Tennessee. He made the decision to get rid of a problematic tree that was located on his property. The solution was to cut the tree down, and this was something Frank was accustomed to. He had cut quite a few trees down throughout his life, and knew all of the precautions to take.

Frank and his Labrador retriever packed up all of their supplies, and headed off to the location of the problematic tree. Once they arrived, Frank secured the tree with a rope. This was to ensure the tree fell in the opposite direction. Frank began to cut the tree down, when the rope that was securing the tree suddenly snapped. As a result, the tree fell back on Frank!

He was now pinned beneath the weight of a massive tree, and was unable to move. Frank was in pain, and knew he needed to get help quickly, as his injuries were severe. Frank had suffered from broken ribs before, and he was certain they were broken this time as well. He didn't have enough air to yell for help.

While he lay there waiting for help to arrive, Henry watched over him. When Frank would nod off, the Labrador Retriever would lick him to keep him awake. Amazingly, by doing this, Henry helped Frank from falling into shock. His cell phone was laying eight feet away, and he couldn't move to get it.

Frank's new neighbors had only moved in weeks ago, but thankfully they emerged from their home to put out the trash. He couldn't yell for help, but Henry knew exactly what to do. As soon as he saw the neighbors, the Labrador Retriever rushed to them and barked uncontrollable. Finally, the man decided to follow him.

Henery led the neighbor to the spot that Frank was lying. Even though The neighbor had never seen Henry before, the Labrador Retriever was not willing to give up. That is why his neighbor felt the urge to find out why Henry was so upset.

A helicopter carried Frank to the Vanderbilt University Medical Center. By the time Frank arrived, he had experienced severe blood loss due to a ruptured spleen. The doctors told Frank's wife he was very close to dying. He wasn't out of danger yet, as his injuries were very serious. Frank had lost a lot of blood, and was facing multiple surgeries. Miraculously, he pulled through and credits Henry for saving his life.

Frank had shattered his arm and leg, ruptured his spleen, cracked seven ribs, and punctured both lungs. Had Henry not kept Frank awake, he may not have survived. Henry has always been attached to

Frank, and this incident proved the bond they share is very tight.

While Frank was in the hospital, The heroic **Labrador Retriever** would look for him around the house. Jane, Frank's wife, said, "Henry waited near the back door to the garage, waiting for Frank to come home. We have a housekeeper who comes on Fridays and Henry just loves her, but she let him outside one day and he just took off smelling all over the yard like he was looking for Frank. He didn't want to come back in."

When Frank made it home, he had to sleep in the recliner for a while. Henry wouldn't let him out of his sight, and slept right next to Frank's recliner. The **Labrador Retriever** continues to look after Frank. There have been a few times that Frank's leg has given out on him. He will call a neighbor to come help him get up. Henry always greets the neighbor in the driveway and shows them where Frank is.

Henry has looked after Frank since he was a puppy. The two of them have been inseparable. Frank believes Henry loves him unconditionally, and shows his love by always being by his side.

<u>Duke</u>

Adopting a dog from the pound or local humane society can be very rewarding. You are saving an animal, and giving them a fair chance at life. Never judge a book by its cover, just because a dog has ended up in a pound doesn't mean they are not worthy of love. There are some really amazing dogs that have come from pounds.

In Portland, Connecticut the Brousseau family adopted their dog Duke from a local animal shelter. Duke is a mixed breed, but has always been very well-behaved. The Brousseau says Duke has been an absolute joy to have in their family.

It was a Saturday night in early October 2012. The Brousseau's were new parents, and had learned that sleeping was a privilege with a newborn baby in their home. They were fast asleep in their beds when suddenly they were awakened by Duke. He was shaking and jumping on the bed. Jenna Brousseau knew something was wrong because Duke never acted this way.

They followed Duke, into the room of their new daughter, Harper, to check on her. When they arrived in her room they found that Harper was not breathing. The Brousseau's quickly called 911, and rushed Harper to the emergency room. The doctors were able to revive Harper, and thanks to Duke she survived. Somehow, he sensed that Harper was in distress and alerted the Brousseau's.

Duke saved nine week old Harper, and returned the favor to the Brousseau's for saving his life six years earlier when they adopted him. They can't say enough good things about their heroic dog Duke. They feel very blessed to have him as part of their family.

Eve, a True Companion

These faithful companions continue to put their owner's lives before their own. They sense danger and seek the help that is needed. In this next story, Eve came to her owner's aid without hesitation. If she had been seconds later it could have costed both of them their lives.

Kathie Vaughan suffers from multiple sclerosis and is a paraplegic. She is paralyzed from the waist down. Multiple sclerosis is an inflammatory disease which affects the central nerve system. She purchased a used truck just hours earlier and was traveling down the road with her trusty companion Eve. Eve is her Rottweiler that goes everywhere Kathie goes.

Driving a truck on a good day could be challenging for Kathie because of her disability, but she valued the privilege of still being able to drive. Being paralyzed had not taken that ability away from her.

Kathie suddenly lost control of her truck. The truck then began to swerve and without warning it began to fishtail. Kathie had to think quickly in order to get the truck to a full stop. With much effort she was finally able to bring the truck to a stop with a loud squeal. Little did she know at that time that was just the beginning of her problems!

The inside of the cab started filling with toxic fumes and black smoke. It was filling quickly. A person without a disability like Kathie could have simply opened the truck door and jump out. But she could not walk. The truck was now on fire and in danger of blowing up at any second. Kathie acted as

quickly as she could. She open the truck door and

pushed Eve out along with her wheelchair. The

smoke hindered her view of the cab and she was not

able to find all the pieces to her wheelchair.

The feeling of terror fell over Kathie. She was

very overwhelmed by the situation at hand. If she did

not get out of the truck soon she was endangered of

losing her life to smoke inhalation or perhaps even an

explosion. In her darkest hour, Kathie was not alone.

Her trusty companion never left her side. Eve sensed

the urgency of the situation and she acted on Kathie's

behalf.

Kathie was near the point of blacking out, when

suddenly she felt Eve's jaws grab her leg. Eve

refused to abandon her loving owner and friend. A

warm sense of relief flooded over her, because she knew that Eve would stay with her no matter what. Eve tightly grabbed her ankles and pulled her ten feet away from the now burning truck.

The truck was in full flames. If Eve had been seconds later, Kathie may have burnt up in her truck. Oblivious to the terrifying fire, Eve continued to drag Kathie to a nearby ditch.

A police officer appeared on the scene as the flames were approaching the gas tank. The policeman shouted, "You've got to get further away" to Kathie. There were only seconds before the truck would explode and would do damage to anything in its path. The officer failed to realize Kathie's disabilities. She continued to struggle pulling herself away from the fire and towards the police car.

Kathie had shooting pains all over her body. The aching was enough to make her want to give into the pain, but she couldn't give up now. Eve had helped her come this far and she was only a few feet from safety. That's when Eve, came to her rescue once again. She bent over so that Kathie could grab onto her collar without difficulty.

Kathie could not believe that her friend was there for her once again. She gasped Eve collar tightly as the heroic dog pulled her forty foot out of harm's way. A fire crew showed up shortly after and spent hours extinguishing the flames.

It was a trying day for Kathie and Eve. Both of them were mentally and physically exhausted from the events that took place. Not only had both of them nearly lost their lives they also realized what a precious bond was between them. Kathie is so thankful that Eve came to rescue that day. Had Eve stood back and watched Kathie would have lost her life.

Eve has been awarded the notable Stillman Award for bravery. She will forever be a hero in Kathie's eyes.

Roselle

September 11, 2001, is a day that will forever be remembered by people around the nation. Thousands of people were affected by the events that unfolded that day as terrorists destroyed the World Trade Center towers in New York.

Sheer terror struck the lives of all Americans. Those who were directly affected by the terrorist, fought for their lives and were willing to do anything to escape the events that were unfolding. Everyone who survived this horrific event can testify that living is a blessing that should not be taken for granted. This story is just one of hundreds who did survive that day.

Michael Hingson was born blind, but has managed to become very successful. He earned his Master's degree in Physics at the University of California. Michael was able to function normally with the help of a guide dog. A prestigious yellow Labrador Retriever would make his fifth guide. They were introduced at the Guide Dogs for the Blind, on November 22, 1999. He could tell that Roselle was a perfect match for him the first time they walked together. Michael knew from the beginning that this Labrador Retriever was special.

He lived a fast paced life in New York City, and worked at the World Trade Center. Each day Roselle accompanied him to his office. She was used to Michael's fast paced life, and was accustomed to leading him where ever he needed to go. September 11, 2001 started out like any other day. Roselle led

Michael to the North Tower of the World Trade

Center, and up to his office on the 78th floor. Michael

was busy working at his desk when he heard a very

large explosion. He was only one of a thousand

people working in the World Trade center that day,

but he was at a huge disadvantage because he

couldn't see anything that was going on.

He knew that something was very wrong, but

he would have to depend on Roselle to be his eyes

during this horrific situation. Roselle had been

sleeping under Michael's desk, but she quickly woke

up when the American Airlines flight 11 hijacked

planes hit the North Tower of the World Trade Center.

Instantly, Roselle sensed the urgency of the situation.

Michael and Roselle would have to work as a

team if they were going to make it down 78 floors of

stairs alive. Michael didn't know how long they had to get out, but he was aware that the building was in danger of collapsing. Knowing that this was a life or death situation he took a minute to call his wife. He said he loved her, and would be in touch as soon as he could. Then, Michael gave Roselle the "Forward" command, and off they went into a smoked filled hallway. For a lead dog, the forward command is one of the first commands that they learn. It basically tells the dog, it's time to work.

Michael grasped her harness tightly, and out of his office they went. In the hall they were faced with large amounts of smoke, noise, and utter confusion. Michael had to fight the urge to panic. He had to put his trust in Roselle and work with her as a team. Amazingly, Roselle remained very calm, though this whole terrifying event. "I would not be alive today if it weren't for Roselle," Michael states with gratitude.

At first the crowds were small, but the further down they went the more the crowds began to grow. The air was filled with smoke and the stairwell was completely black. The heat was intensifying to temperatures over 90 degrees, which made it very difficult to breathe. Michael was pouring sweat and Roselle was panting very heavily. The odor from the fumes of the jet fuel continued to increase.

People were moving at a fast pace down the stairwell. Michael became increasingly worried about Roselle because she was panting so hard. He knew she needed a drink. When they finally reached the lobby a lot of pipes were spraying water. Michael gave Roselle a command to stop and take a drink. It took Michael and Roselle a total of 50 minutes to make it to the ground floor, and another 10 minutes to make it outside to the street. In order to get to fresh air and freedom, they descended a total of 1,463 stairs, through the most extreme conditions.

The terror didn't stop once they were outside. There was total chaos in the streets of New York City. Michael heard the sound of the second tower collapsing. People all around him screamed in fear, but amazingly Roselle still remained calm. Together, they made their way to the subway. When they finally emerged from the subway, the streets of New York City were covered in soot and debris.

Through it all Michael and Roselle remained a team. They worked together to make it out alive. Roselle is a true hero because she never swayed from the task at hand. This brave Labrador Retriever remained calm, and did as Michael commanded. Michael was later quoted saying, "sometimes being a hero is just doing your job." And that is exactly what Roselle did!

Book's By Jennifer Ogden

Coming Soon!

Hero Dog Stories Volume 2: More Amazing Tales of

Love and Courage

This Who I Am: Poetry Collection

Other Book's By Jennifer Ogden

Jennifer Ogden's
Learning with Friends Series
Available Now on Amazon

Come along on this exciting

rhyming adventure of learning how

to count!

Join our friends to learn each letter.

A new letter is introduced on each

page with a new friend.

Learning Colors with Friends

By: Jennifer Ogden

Each friend has a new color for you to learn.

Other Childrens Books by Jennifer Ogden

Ann has a plan. She recruits the help of her friend Fran. This is the story of how their cupcake production began.

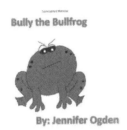

Bully is a mean Bullfrog, but Earl and Penny are determined to change his ways.

Princess Bedtime Stories has 9 original princess stories for kids!

The Gaudian Series

Ivan must prepare the creatures of Whispering Pines for the battle against Boldyn.

Join the Guardian and the creatures of Whispering Pines as they battle the evil Boldwyn to save their home.

About The Author

My passion comes from the words I pour upon a page. Writing is something that has carried me through my life, and it fills me with joy each time a reader hears my voice. Hidden in the depths of my words is so much more than what meets the eye.

I am a small town girl who enjoys the simple things in life. I have been blessed with two beautiful children and a wonderful husband. My writing obsession started in fourth grade, and it has now become my full time job. I wake each morning overjoyed knowing that I get to share my passion with the world. It is my belief that if you truly love what you do for a living, you never have to work a day in your life.

Well, I must confess, I'm living a dream. I started my career in 2013. I have managed to become a successful Freelance Creative Writer and Author. I hope one day to travel the world, and inspire people with the words that I write. The minute I stop wishing and started believing my dream became reality. When you believe you can do it, amazing things will happen.

Recommended Books about Dogs

Want to read another book about dogs? Here are some great books about dogs that you may like:

Because of Winn Dixie by Kate DiCamillo

Shiloh by Phyllis Reynolds Naylor

Racing in the Rain by Garth Stein

If Only I Could Talk: A Canine Adventure by Tony Lewis

Ribsy by Beverly Cleary

Lucky Phoo by Stacia Deutsch and Rhody Cohon

22994797R00079

Printed in Great Britain
by Amazon